SCALES
& ARPEGGIOS

FOR VIOLIN

for students preparing for
all examinations of the

ROYAL ACADEMY OF MUSIC
and the

ROYAL COLLEGE OF MUSIC

Order No: NOV915302

PAXTON MUSIC

Scales and Arpeggios for the Violin

CONTENTS

Paxton

15302

Section 1

Major and Minor Scales in Two Octaves

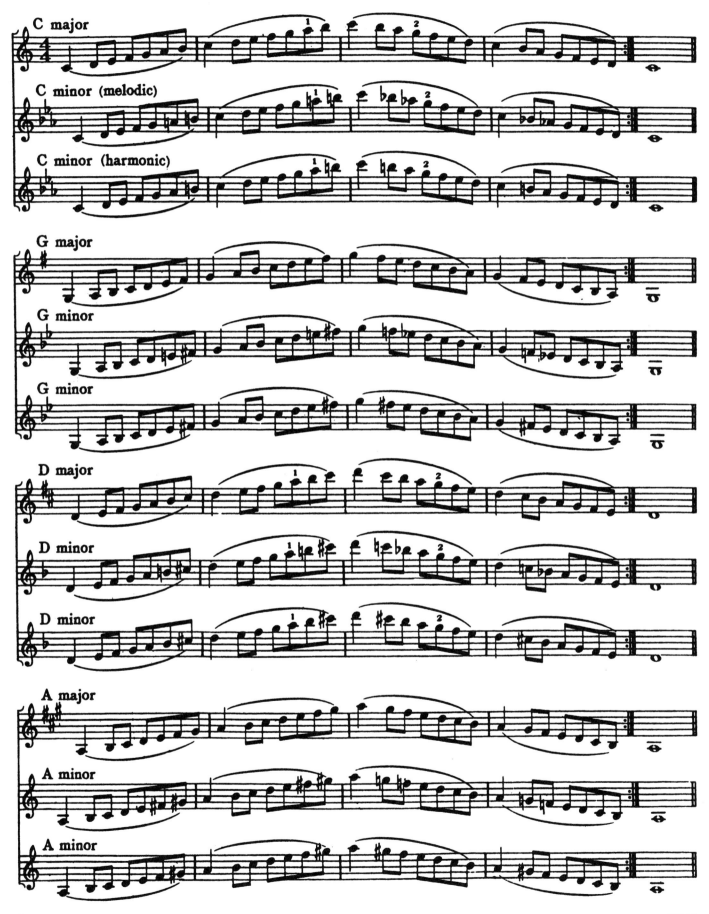

C major

C minor (melodic)

C minor (harmonic)

G major

G minor

G minor

D major

D minor

D minor

A major

A minor

A minor

Paxton

2

E major

E minor

E minor

B major

B minor

B minor

F# major (enharmonic Gb)

F# minor

F# minor

Db major (enharmonic C#)

C# minor

C# minor

15302

A♭ major

A♭ minor (enharmonic G♯ minor)

A♭ minor

E♭ major

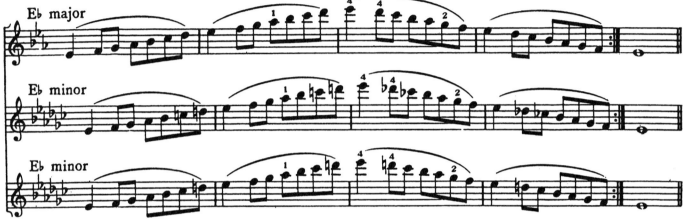

E♭ minor

E♭ minor

B♭ major

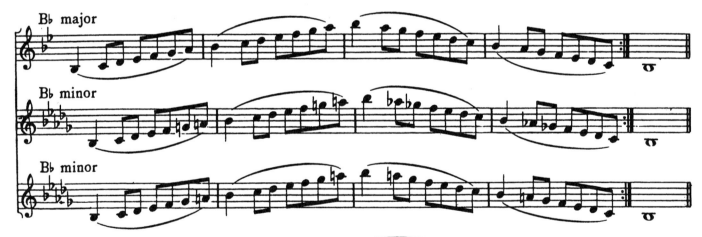

B♭ minor

B♭ minor

F major

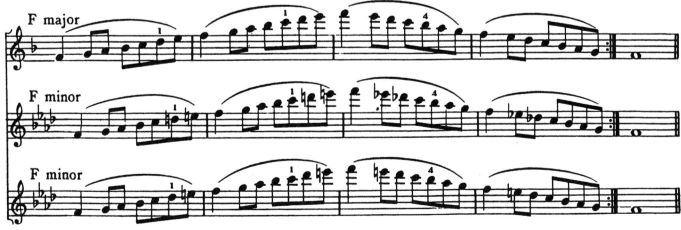

F minor

F minor

Paxton

15302

4

Chromatic Scales in Two Octaves

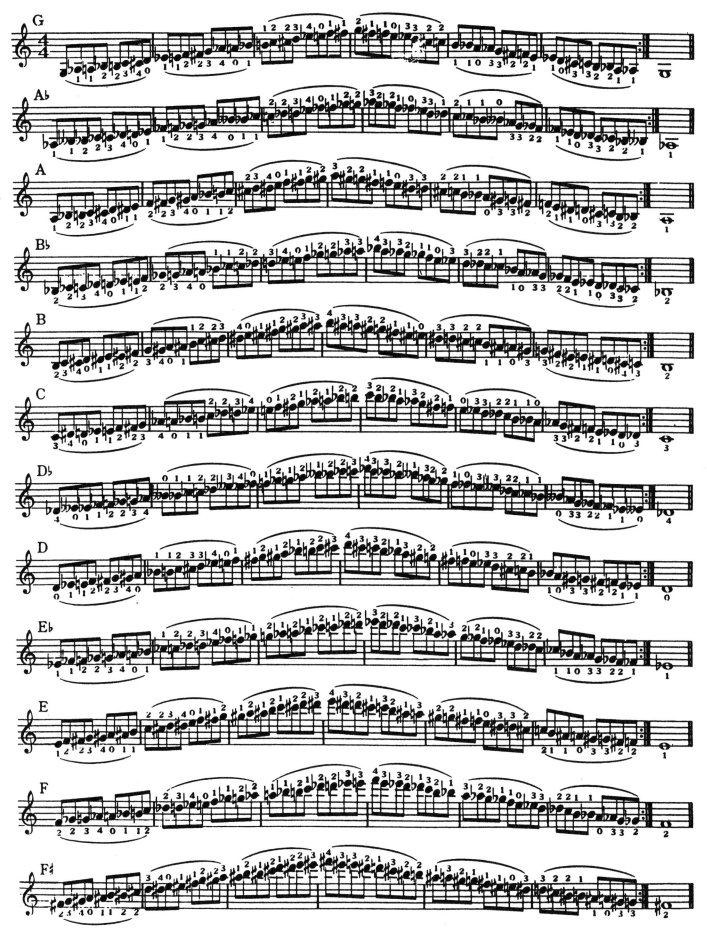

Arpeggios of Common Chords in Two Octaves

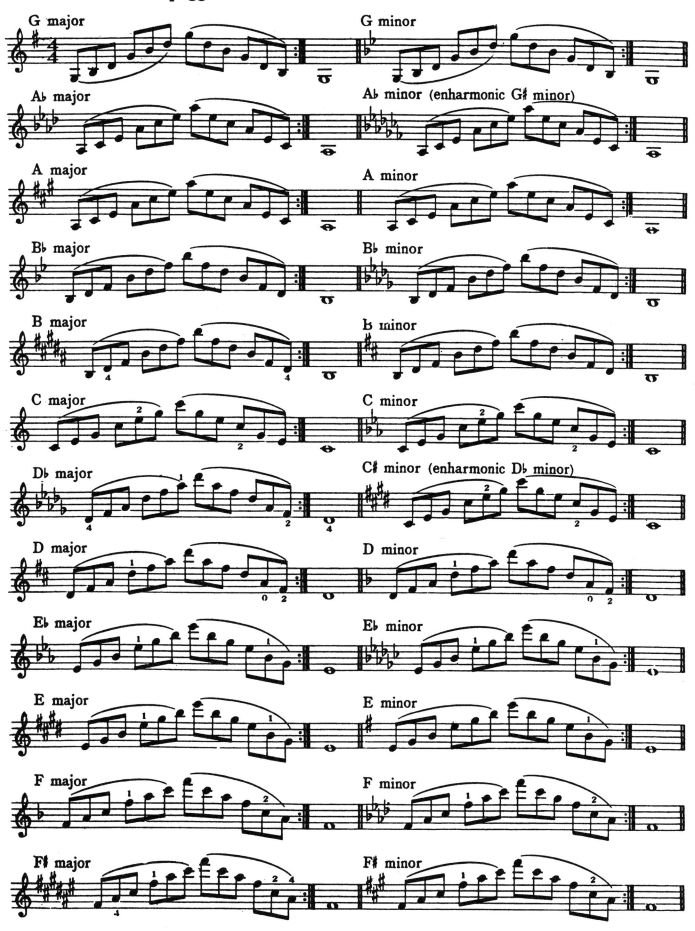

Arpeggios of Dominant Sevenths in Two Octaves

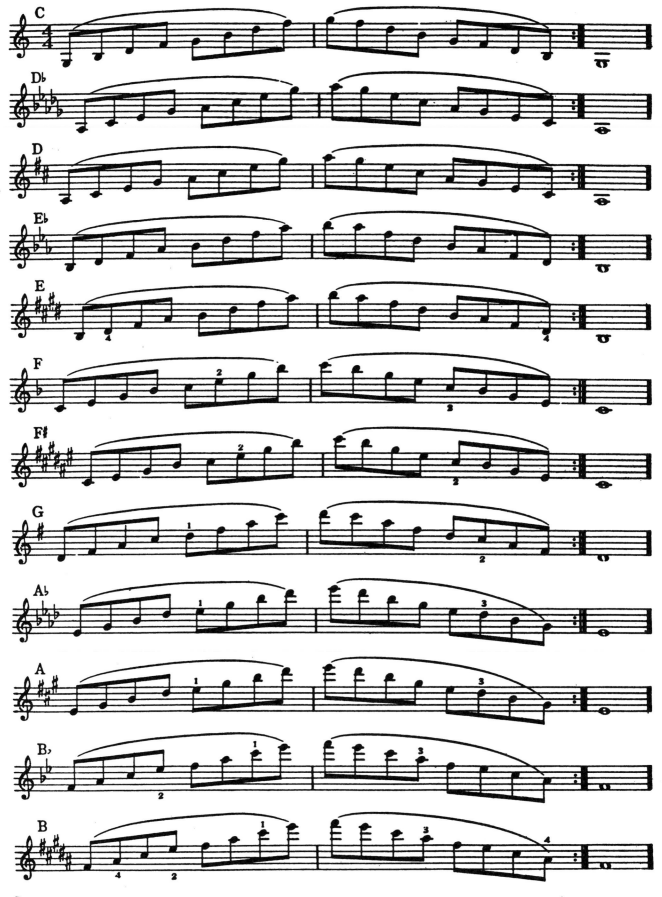

15302

Arpeggios of Diminished Sevenths in Two Octaves

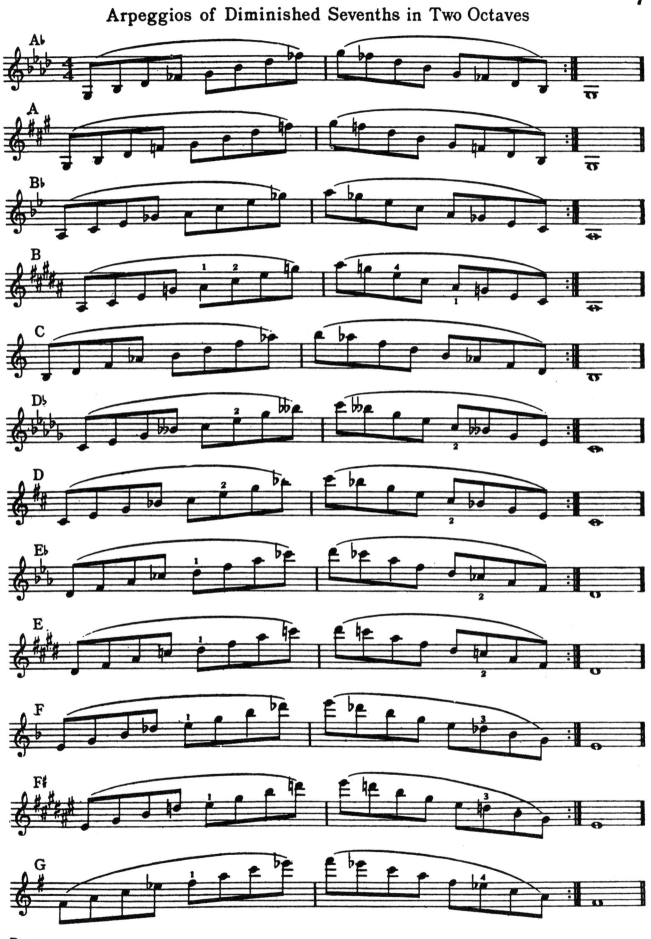

Paxton

15392

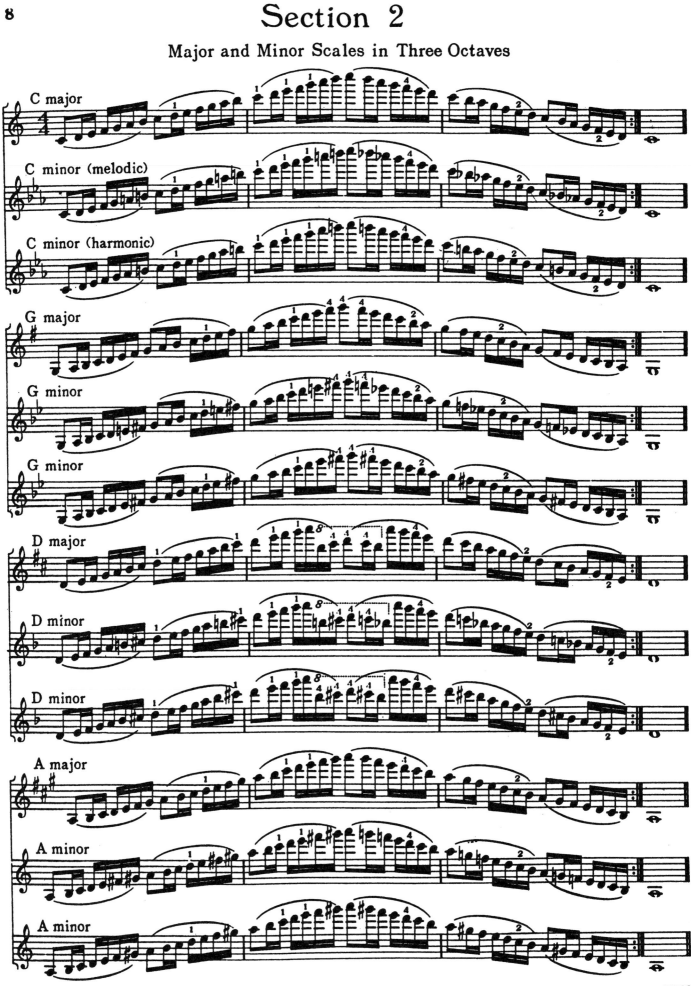

Section 2
Major and Minor Scales in Three Octaves

C major

C minor (melodic)

C minor (harmonic)

G major

G minor

G minor

D major

D minor

D minor

A major

A minor

A minor

Paxton

15302

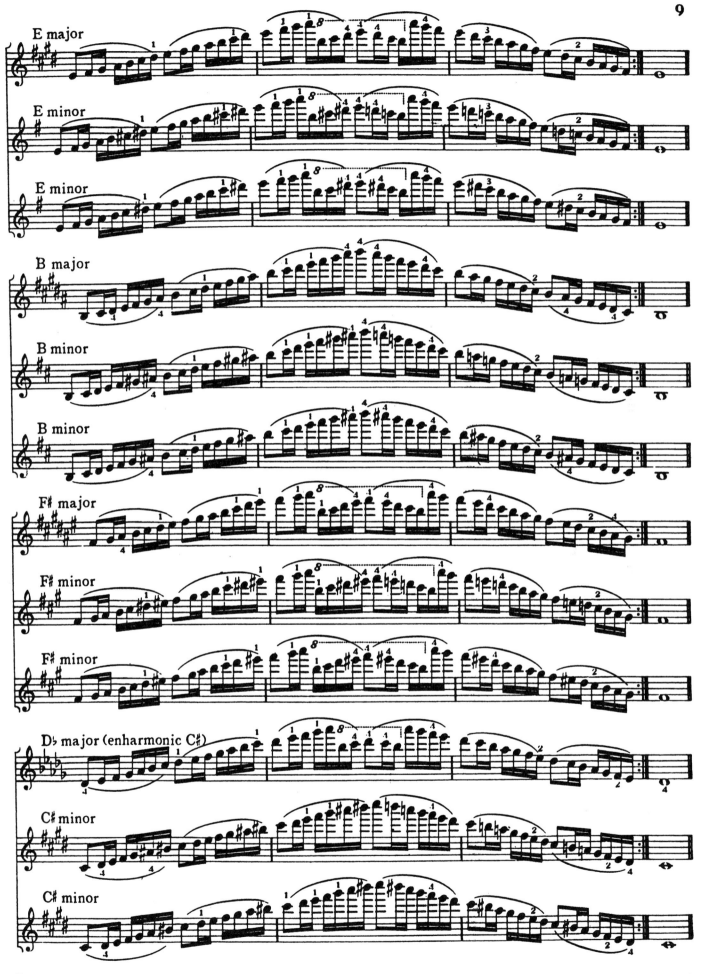

15302

10

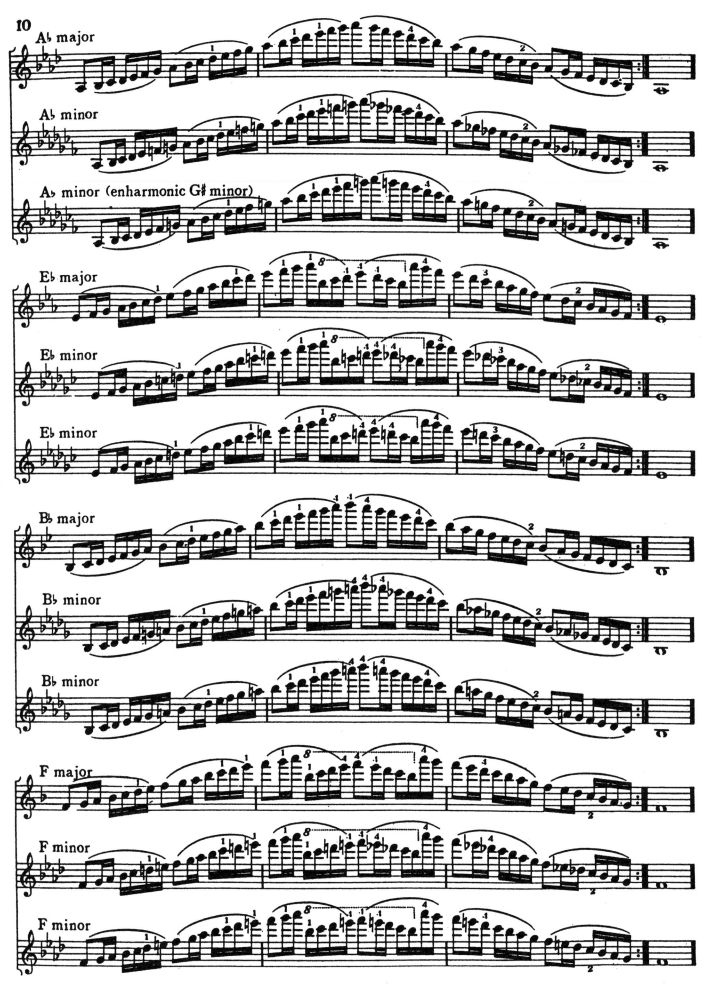

Arpeggios of Common Chords in Three Octaves

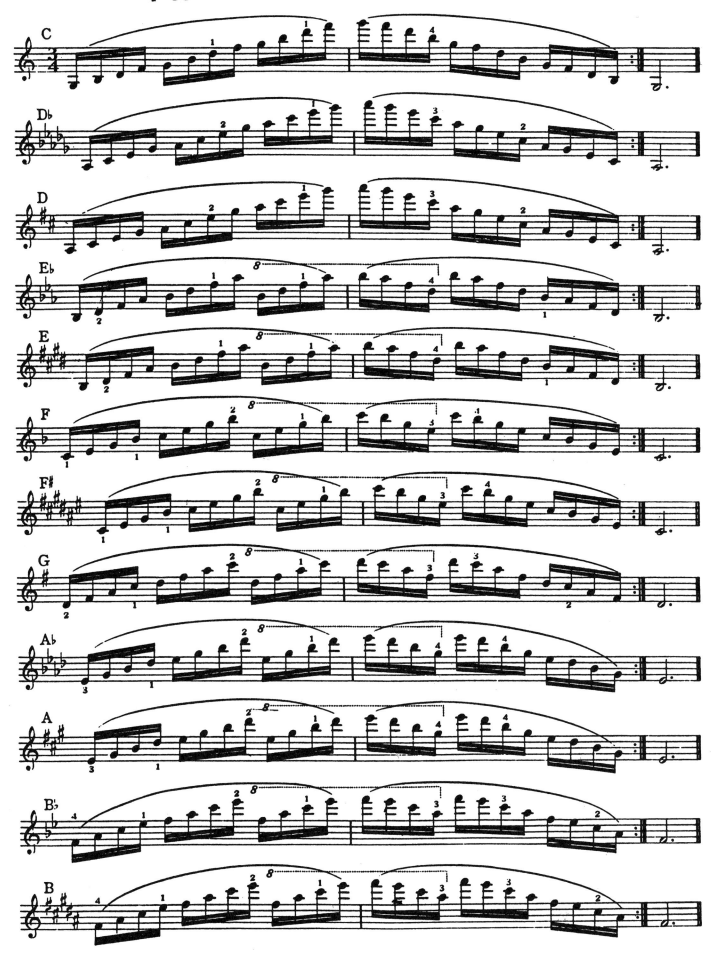

Paxton

Arpeggios of Diminished Sevenths in Three Octaves.

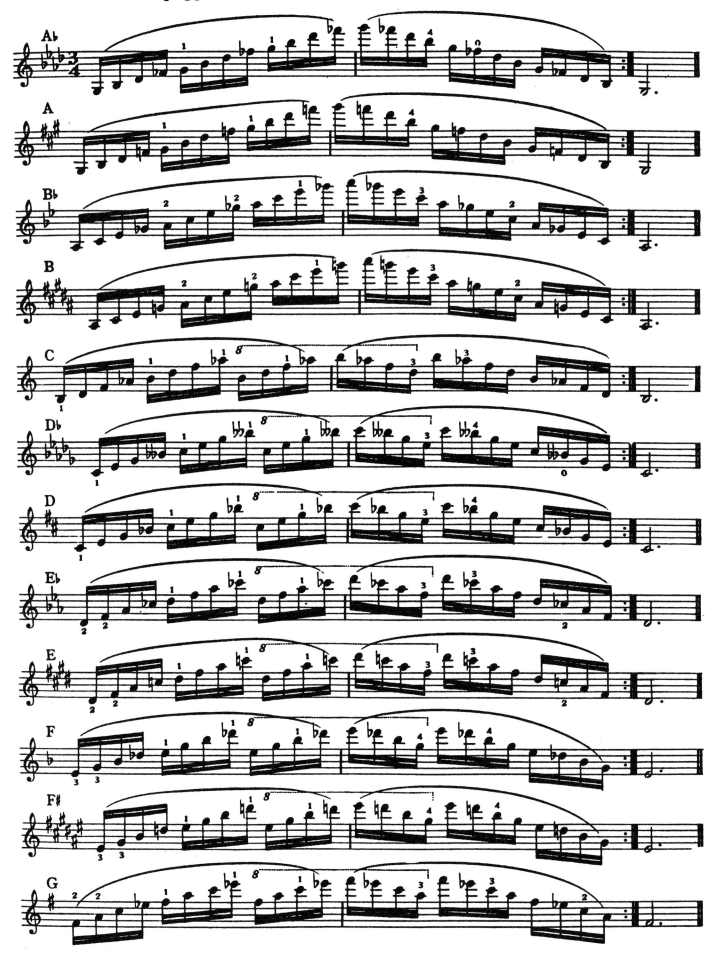

15302

Section 3

Major and Minor Scales in Thirds

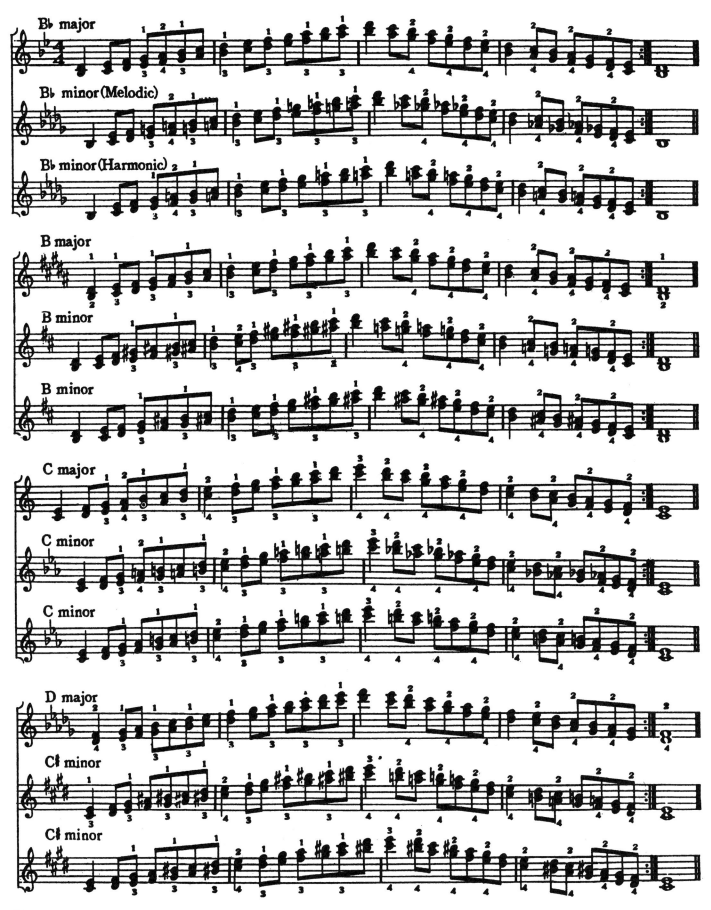

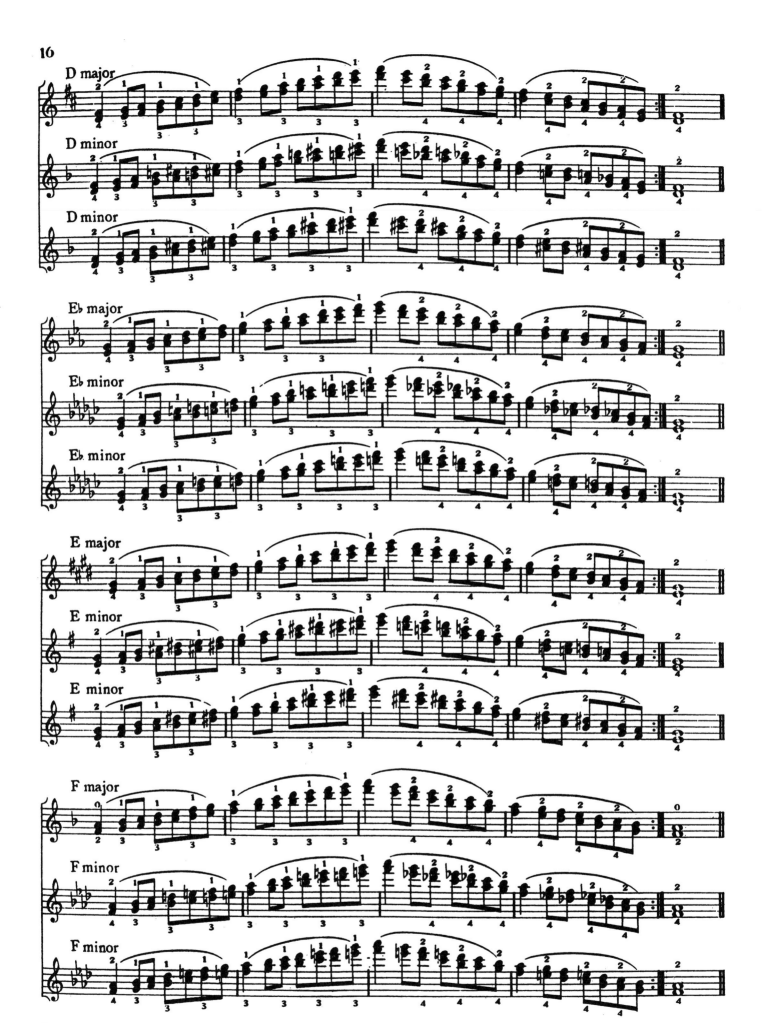

15302

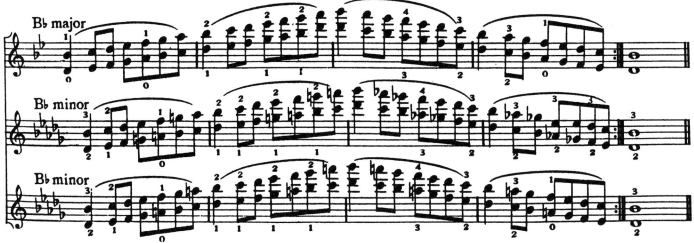

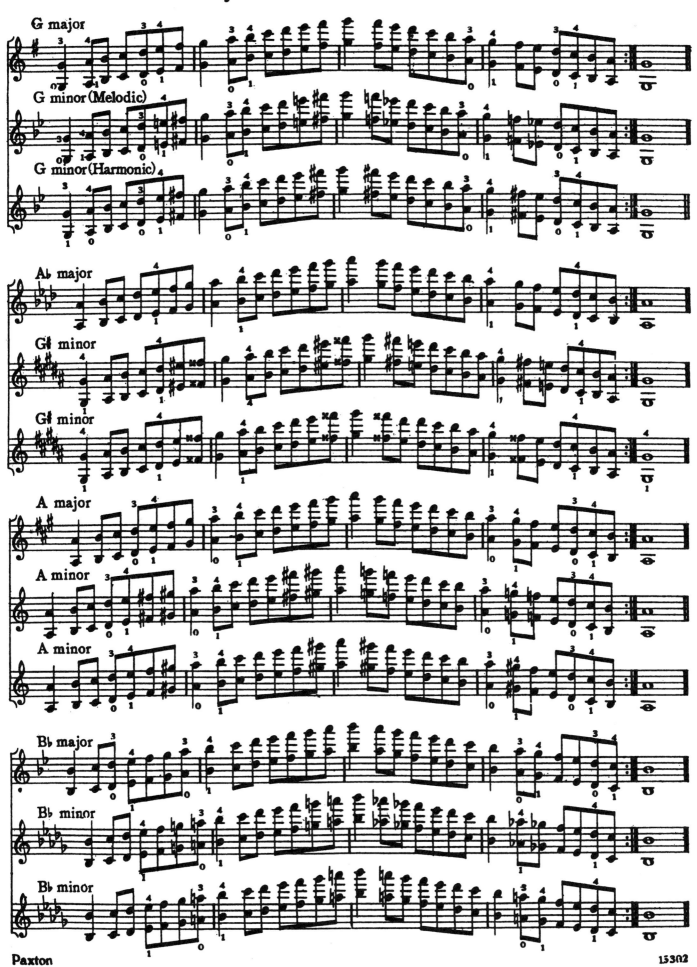

20

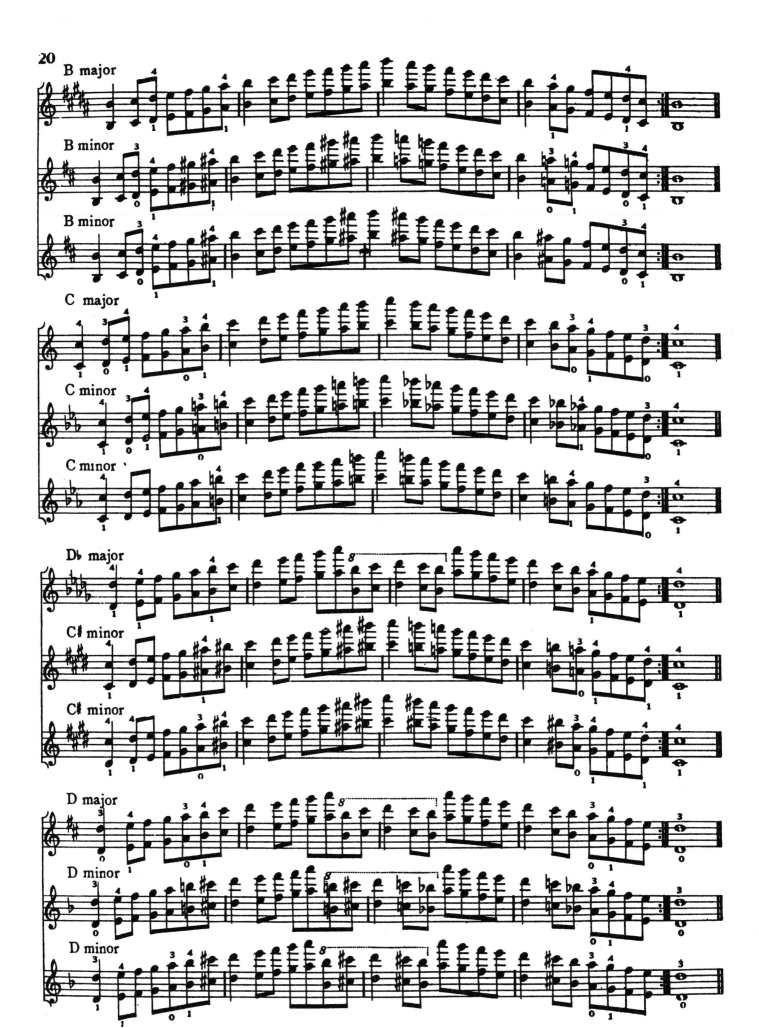

15302

21

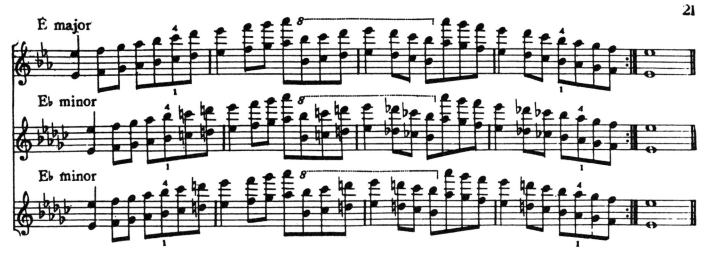

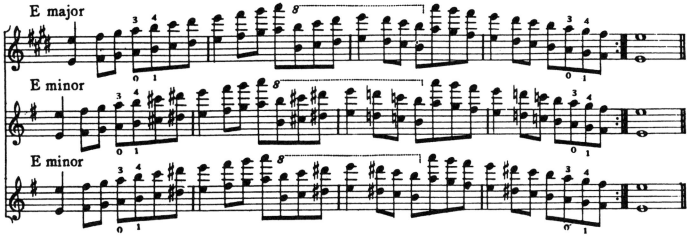